**1**

# Pyramids

## Laura Marsh

Washington, D.C.

# For young explorers everywhere —L.F.M.

Trade paperback ISBN: 978-1-4263-2690-5
Reinforced library binding ISBN: 978-1-4263-2691-2

The author and publisher gratefully acknowledge the expert content review of this book by Jennifer Houser Wegner, Ph.D., associate curator, Egyptian Section, Penn Museum, and the literacy review of this book by Mariam Jean Dreher, professor of reading education, University of Maryland, College Park.

**Photo Credits**

Cover, WitR/Getty Images; Vocabulary boxes, Andy Vinnikov/Shutterstock; top border, scigelova/Shutterstock; 1 (CTR), NurPhoto/Getty Images; 3 (LO), Rahmo/Shutterstock; 4-5 (CTR), sculpies/Shutterstock; 6 (LO), Holbox/Shutterstock; 7 (CTR), Tor Eigeland/Alamy Stock Photo; 8 (CTR), Waj/Shutterstock; 9 (UP), ClassicStock/Masterfile; 10 (UP), Everett Historical/Shutterstock; 10 (CTR), Brian Maudsley/Shutterstock; 10 (LO), Interfoto/Alamy Stock Photo; 11 (UP), Rue des Archives/Granger, NYC—All rights reserved; 11 (CTR), Mikkel Juul Jensen/Science Photo Library; 11 (LO), Peter Phipp/Travelshots.com/Alamy Stock Photo; 12-13 (RT), O. Louis Mazzatenta/National Geographic Creative; 14 (UP), Phas/Getty Images; 15 (CTR RT), Kenneth Garrett/National Geographic Creative; 15 (CTR LE), S. Vannini/Getty Images; 15 (LO), RobertHarding/Masterfile; 16 (LE), Marc Deville/Getty Images; 17 (CTR), Mikhail Zahranichny/Shutterstock; 18-19 (RT), Granger.com—All rights reserved; 20 (LO), Mary Evans Picture Library/Alamy Stock Photo; 21 (CTR), travelpixs/Alamy Stock Photo; 22 (LO), Everett Historical/Shutterstock; 23 (UP), GL Archive/Alamy Stock Photo; 24 (LO), Everett Collection Historical/Alamy Stock Photo; 25 (CTR), Kenneth Garrett/National Geographic Creative; 26 (CTR), Brando Quilici; 27 (CTR), Vladimir Wrangel/Shutterstock; 27 (LO), Claus Lunau/Science Photo Library; 28 (LO), Cengage/National Geographic Creative; 29 (UP), Cengage/National Geographic Creative; 30 (LO LE), Marc Deville/Getty Images; 30 (LO RT), Martin Gray/National Geographic Creative; 31 (UP LE), S. Vannini/Getty Images; 31 (UP RT), Robert Harding/Alamy Stock Photo; 31 (LO LE), Universal Images Group/Getty Images; 31 (LO RT), Anna Stowe Travel/Alamy Stock Photo; 32 (UP LE), Marc Deville/Getty Images; 32 (UP RT), Tor Eigeland/Alamy Stock Photo; 32 (LO LE), Stanislaw Tokarski/Shutterstock; 32 (LO RT), travelpixs/Alamy Stock Photo

National Geographic supports K–12 educators with ELA Common Core Resources. Visit natgeoed.org/commoncore for more information.

Printed in the United States of America
21/WOR/2

# Table of Contents

Great Pyramids                        4

Big Buildings                         6

6 Cool Facts About Pyramids          10

Home in the Afterlife                12

Making Mummies                       16

Inside a Pyramid                     18

Robbers                              20

King Tut's Tomb                      22

Still Exploring                      26

What in the World?                   30

Glossary                             32

# Great Pyramids

The pyramids in Giza, Egypt, were built 4,500 years ago.

What is topped with a point,
And reaches way up high?

What is built from stone,
With room for a mummy inside?

A pyramid (PEER-uh-mid)!

## Egypt Word

**PYRAMID:** A triangle shape with four sides and a square base

# Big Buildings

Pyramids are found in many places. The most famous pyramids are in Giza (GEE-za), Egypt. They are huge. Long ago, ancient Egyptian (AYN-shunt ee-JIP-shun) rulers were buried inside them.

This is a Maya pyramid in Mexico. There are pyramids in Central America and other places, too.

In Giza, the largest pyramid is called the Great Pyramid.

The Giza Pyramids are made of stone blocks. Each block weighs more than a big family car.

One stone block would come up to the shoulder of most men.

Scientists think it took about 20 years to build the Great Pyramid. Workers may have used ropes and ramps.

Building the pyramids was hard work. Thousands of people moved the blocks into place.

# 6 COOL FACTS About Pyramids

**1** The first pyramid in Egypt was called the Step Pyramid. It was built in Saqqara (SAH-ka-rah) more than 4,600 years ago. Pyramids with smooth sides came later.

**2** The Giza Pyramids had smooth sides when they were built. An outer layer of smooth stone covered the pyramids. Today the outer layer has mostly worn away.

**3** It took about 20,000 workers to build the Great Pyramid, the largest pyramid in Giza.

**4** The Great Pyramid was built with more than two million stone blocks.

**5** Some stone blocks were brought by boat on the Nile River. But many blocks came from an area near the Great Pyramid.

**6** The Eiffel Tower in Paris, France, became the tallest building in the world in 1889. Before that, the Great Pyramid was the tallest.

# Home in the Afterlife

Ancient Egyptian rulers were called pharaohs (FAIR-ohs). People believed pharaohs lived on after they died. This was called the afterlife.

A pyramid was built for the pharaoh's body. It protected the body for the afterlife.

In this wall painting, Egyptians prepare a body for the afterlife.

13

It took workers many hours to prepare a pharaoh's tomb.

The pyramid was the pharaoh's tomb (TOOM). People filled it with things the pharaoh would need in the next life.

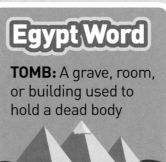

**Egypt Word**

TOMB: A grave, room, or building used to hold a dead body

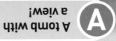
Food and furniture were put inside. Jewelry and weapons were put in, too. The tombs held many treasures (TREZH-urs).

These are treasures from a pharaoh's tomb—a hawk, a piece of jewelry, and a painted box.

15

# Making Mummies

When a pharaoh died, the body was made into a mummy. Salts, oils, and perfumes were put on the body.

Next the mummy was wrapped with strips of cloth. Then it was put into a coffin.

a mummy

## Egypt Word

**MUMMY:** A dead body that is treated and prepared for burial with strips of cloth

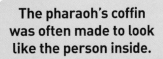

The pharaoh's coffin was often made to look like the person inside.

# Inside a Pyramid

A pyramid often had several rooms inside. The pharaoh's coffin was placed in the burial (BEAR-ee-ul) room.

This room was in the middle of the pyramid. A long, narrow tunnel led to it.

More tunnels led to other rooms. Treasures were kept there, too. Some pyramids had burial chambers hidden below the pyramid.

an entrance to a tunnel in the Great Pyramid

19

# Robbers

Long ago, people robbed the pyramids. They dug through the stone. They stole the treasures inside. So pharaohs needed a new kind of tomb. The time of the pyramids was over.

In this illustration, a tomb is discovered. But robbers have already been there.

Instead, the pharaohs built hidden tombs. The tombs were cut into cliffs or buried below the earth. But most of those tombs were robbed, too.

the entrance to a pharaoh's tomb today in Valley of the Kings, Luxor, Egypt

# King Tut's Tomb

Robbers and explorers found many tombs. By the 1900s, most tombs had been found. But the tomb of one king had not—King Tut.

art showing King Tut and his wife

22

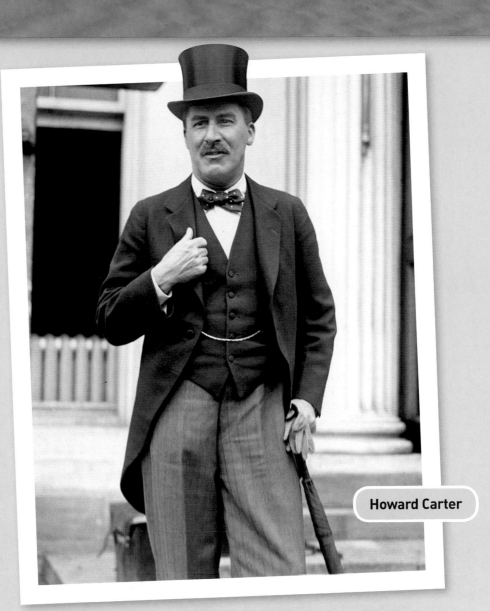

Howard Carter

A man named Howard Carter
tried to find Tut's tomb.
He searched for many years.

In 1922, Carter found hidden steps to a burial room. Rocks from another tomb had covered it.

Inside was the tomb of King Tut! Carter found a lot of treasures. They were more than 3,000 years old.

Howard Carter studies King Tut's coffin.

This golden mask covered the mummy of King Tut.

# Still Exploring

A scientist uses a machine to scan the walls in the tomb.

People are still exploring pyramids and tombs. In 2015, scientists said there might be hidden rooms in Tut's tomb! They used new radar scans to find them.

They thought the tomb of Queen Nefertiti (NEF-er-TEE-tee) might be inside!

Queen Nefertiti was the famous wife of King Tut's father.

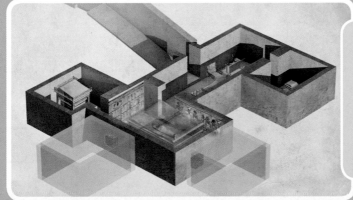

This computer drawing shows a map of King Tut's tomb. The rooms in shadows are possible rooms not yet discovered.

Many more lost tombs and pyramids are buried in the ground. Sarah Parcak has a new way to find them.

Sarah Parcak is at work in the field.

Parcak studies a satellite photo.

She looks at satellite (SAT-uh-lite) photos of Earth. They show where things may be under the ground. She has found hundreds of places to search. Maybe she will find new tombs and pyramids to explore!

**Egypt Word**

SATELLITE: A spacecraft that gathers information

# What in the World?

These pictures show up-close views of things having to do with pyramids. Use the hints to figure out what's in the pictures. Answers are on page 31.

**1**

**HINT:** a body wrapped in cloth

**2**

**HINT:** Pyramids are built with these.

# Word Bank

satellite   tunnel   pharaoh   **Great Pyramid**   mummy   stone blocks

**3**

**HINT:** an Egyptian ruler

**4**

**HINT:** a long, narrow
path inside a pyramid

**5**

**HINT:** Sarah Parcak uses
these kinds of photos.

**6**

**HINT:** the largest
Giza Pyramid

Answers: 1. mummy, 2. stone blocks, 3. pharaoh, 4. tunnel, 5. satellite, 6. Great Pyramid

**MUMMY:** A dead body that is treated and prepared for burial with strips of cloth

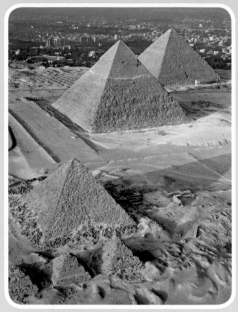

**PYRAMID:** A triangle shape with four sides and a square base

**SATELLITE:** A spacecraft that gathers information

**TOMB:** A grave, room, or building used to hold a dead body